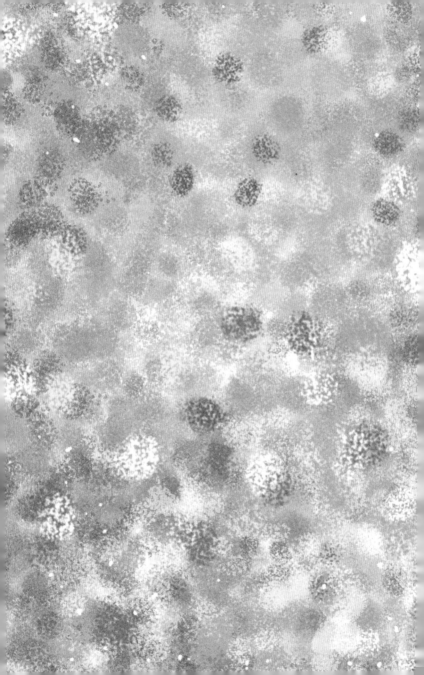

You are truly one of a kind,
and you deserve a beautiful day
and a wonderful year ahead.

— Kim Lynn Price

We wish to thank the following authors and authors' representatives for permission to reprint the following poems that appear in this publication: PrimaDonna Entertainment Corp. for "You are a treasure to me..." and "Bless you for being you..." by Donna Fargo. Copyright © 2002, 2015 by PrimaDonna Entertainment Corp. All rights reserved. And Candy Paull for "In you, I see courage and strength...." Copyright © 2012 by Candy Paull. All rights reserved.

ISBN: 978-1-68088-409-8

◪ and Blue Mountain Press are registered in U.S. Patent and Trademark Office. Certain trademarks are used under license.

Printed in China.
First Printing: 2022

♲ This book is printed on recycled paper.

This book is printed on paper that has been specially produced to be acid free (neutral pH) and contains no groundwood or unbleached pulp. It conforms with the requirements of the American National Standards Institute, Inc., so as to ensure that this book will last and be enjoyed by future generations.

Blue Mountain Arts, Inc.

P.O. Box 4549, Boulder, Colorado 80306

Happy Birthday to You!

I hope you feel enormously appreciated today... because you are

A Blue Mountain Arts® Collection

Edited by Becky McKay

Blue Mountain Press™

Boulder, Colorado

Your Birthday
Is the Perfect Time
to Appreciate
and Celebrate the
Wonderful Person
You Are!

celebrate

amazing

Birthdays are a gentle reminder
that true happiness comes from
being able to love and accept
the amazing and miraculous person you are.
You live your life
with purpose and passion
and embrace each and every change.

With each passing year,
you make the world a happier place...
so today, I celebrate the person you are.

— Carlotta Wagner Watson

happiness

You are a treasure to me. A treasure is something really special... something irreplaceable, something you wouldn't want to lose for anything... something you value highly, hold close to your heart, protect and appreciate so much. And since it's your birthday, I want you to know what a treasure you are to me.

I think birthdays are the perfect time to remind those we care about how much they mean to us. So even though words seem inadequate, this is my way of saying...

I hope you have the best day of your life. I hope you have everything you want and need today, and, after that, may each day get better. I send this message with lots of love because... you are a treasure to me.

— Donna Fargo

How to Have
a Great Birthday

Celebrate the sun shining on you
and do something special
just for you.
Take a step in the direction
of making all your dreams
come true.
Have a great time
and spend some moments
with your friends.
Know that the important
things in life
never end.
Take a ride down a rainbow
or wish on a star.

dreams   moments

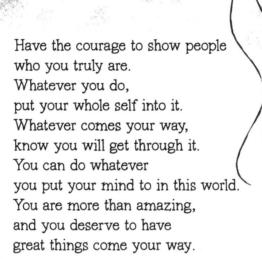

Have the courage to show people
who you truly are.
Whatever you do,
put your whole self into it.
Whatever comes your way,
know you will get through it.
You can do whatever
you put your mind to in this world.
You are more than amazing,
and you deserve to have
great things come your way.

— Ashley Rice

friends

You're the kind of person
who is a true delight
    to know.

Your caring and generous heart
    spills over to everyone you encounter.
You go out of your way to make others
    feel good about themselves.
You're truly a gem —
you shine love and strength
    in all you do.

caring

generous

That's why your birthday should be
    a day of rejoicing —
a day to celebrate the wonder
    of who you are.

I hope your heart is filled with joy
and that you know just how much
    you mean to me and to so many.

You are truly one of a kind,
and you deserve a beautiful day
    and a wonderful year ahead.

— Kim Lynn Price

delight

I'd Love to Give You These Birthday Gifts...

Joy that shines on you along
    every path you walk
Faith to guide you so you
    never feel lost
Hope to keep you positive
    and strong
Peace — so you can hear the
    songs that sing in your heart
Sunshine to dry any tears
Childlike wonder to have and
    hold in your eyes, heart, and soul
A wealth of good friends to
    show you and tell you how much you
    mean to the world
Simple pleasures to celebrate
    and remember

Energy to leap for your highest dreams
Confidence in your talents and
    your power to attract success
Courage to stick to your principles
Respect for your feelings, needs,
    and dreams
Laughter wherever your spirit travels
Family connections that nurture,
    protect, encourage, and help you
    flourish as an individual
Adventures that widen your horizons
Love that comes with all these other
    wishes that are in my heart for you

— Jacqueline Schiff

What Makes a Birthday Truly Special?

Some birthdays are special
because they are milestones.
Whether the 1st or the 21st,
the 40th or the 100th,
each one only happens
once in a lifetime.

Sometimes the birthday party
is what makes the event
unforgettable —
the gathering of people
to share your special day,
the setting, the cake,
the decorations, the music.

All these things maximize
the happy time.
But do you really want to know
what makes a birthday special?

unforgettabl

It's honoring someone
as wonderful as you.

— Connie Anzalone

party honor

milestone

When I look at you, I see someone who is such a kindhearted person. You make everything brighter for everyone around you, and you touch people's lives in a really meaningful and truly beautiful way.

I know you don't get to hear all the words of gratitude and praise you deserve for all you do.

But I want you to remember that you are celebrated and thanked and appreciated more than you'll ever know.

— L. N. Mallory

"Special" is a word that is used
to describe something one of a kind,
like a hug or a sunset
or a person who spreads love
with a smile or kind gesture.
"Special" describes people
who act from the heart
and keep in mind the hearts of others.
"Special" applies to something
that is admired and precious
and that can never be replaced.
"Special" is the word that best
describes you.

— Teri Fernandez

Special

Your Birthday Is Just the Beginning of a Great Year

A birthday isn't just about a particular day. It's about people — family and friends, the love they share, and the happiness in their lives.

A birthday marks a day on the calendar, but it also signifies something special in new experiences and changes. Every year says, "There's so much more ahead, so much more to live." And every year solidifies the love that never stops growing but always keeps giving and living on forever.

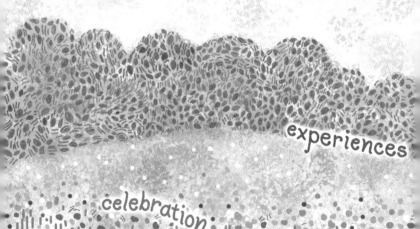

experiences

celebration

A birthday is a one-day celebration for the three hundred sixty-five days waiting in line. It's a kick-start to a lot of days of living and a lot of times to be grateful for. Birthdays are wonderful... enjoy yours today!

— Debbie Burton-Peddle

It's your day to enjoy
    however you want —
to celebrate with friends and family
or sit alone and smile as you remember
such a great past year.
It's a day to love the fact
that you are living this wonderful life —
filled with such amazing people
and perfect moments that make you smile —
and that your life just keeps
getting better every year.

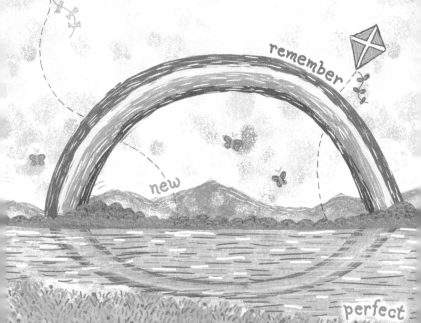

remember

new

perfect

It's a day to forget about
all your worries and all the things
you think you should change
and realize it is a new year for you today —
a year to make what you want it to be.

Enjoy making your next year
better than the last.
Know that today is just
the first day of loving your life
each and every moment.

— Sharlyn Fellenz

The Five Things You Absolutely Have to Do on Your Birthday

wonderful ♫

1. Don't forget how important you are. This day has been marked on my calendar with enough circles and stars and happy feelings to help light up the whole year!

2. Don't ever say to yourself, "This birthday is no big deal; it's just another day." Believe me: this is <u>much</u> <u>more</u> than just another day. Your birthday is everything a celebration should be, because it's in honor of a <u>very</u> <u>special</u> <u>person</u>!

3. Don't forget to do something nice for yourself. Something that will give you a smile — like the ones you always give to everyone else!

4. Don't spend <u>any</u> part of this day worrying about major life decisions. Let the day be carefree. Let it be as happy as a carnival and as much fun as a kaleidoscope. Keep all your options open. (If you can't quite decide between double-Dutch chocolate cake OR poppy seed cake with raspberry filling... have them both!)

5. And don't make just a <u>little</u> wish when you blow out the candles on your cake. Dream big! Have high hopes and happy wishes, and have faith that they'll do their very best to come true... for one very wonderful person: you.

— Douglas Pagels

Some people are so special
that even the sound of their name
lights up our hearts
and brings smiles to our faces.
They are the beautiful souls
who come into our lives
and kindle something so precious
    inside of us.
They add a touch of grace
to the world around them
that lifts the spirits of others.
They aren't afraid to come alongside
and share what they've learned
    and are learning.
This willingness and openness
    of their hearts sets them apart.

soul

genuine

That genuine desire to connect —
to share their love
with the people around them —
is remarkable and life-giving.

You are a beautiful soul,
and I am thankful for you.

— Star Nakamoto

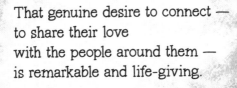

A Birthday Blessing
...Just for You

Bless you for being you. Bless you for inspiring others with your kindness and for caring enough to lift people up and accept them without judgment.

Bless you for your compassion, consistency, and understanding. You believe the best of others. You live your life by example and practice the Golden Rule.

Bless you for celebrating every triumph, for consoling and comforting and sharing the pain of those who hurt. There is no ill will in your heart, no room for selfishness or resentment. You guide and enlighten, and you bring out the good in others.

courage

blessing

Bless you for your strength and perseverance. In the face of adversity, your courage embodies wisdom, humanity, dignity, and a spirit of inclusiveness.

May your rewards be great, and may all the love you give out be returned to you. May you continue to be a bright light of hope and positive energy in this crazy, mixed-up world.

May God's richest blessings be yours on your birthday and every day.

— Donna Fargo

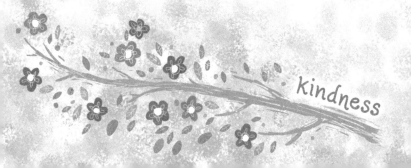

kindness

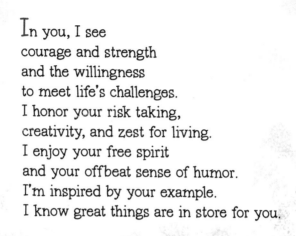

In you, I see
courage and strength
and the willingness
to meet life's challenges.
I honor your risk taking,
creativity, and zest for living.
I enjoy your free spirit
and your offbeat sense of humor.
I'm inspired by your example.
I know great things are in store for you.

creativity

strength

May this birthday be a celebration
of who you are,
what you have done,
and all the amazing potential
that is yet to be realized.
You deserve the very best
life has to offer.

— Candy Paull

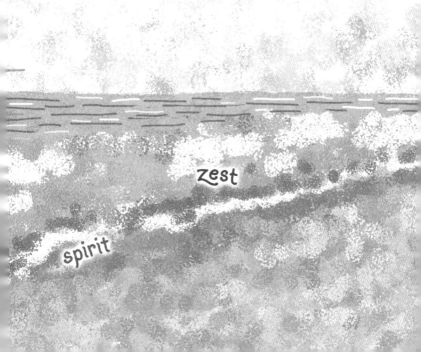

Ten Things
I Wish for You
on Your Birthday

1. That you have fun doing
   all the things you love to do.

2. That you have a smile
   on your face the whole time.

3. That all of your wishes
   come true.

4. That you are loved and cared for.

5. That you get to see your friends
   and laugh with them.

happiest

6. That you get closer to achieving your dreams.

7. That hope smiles at your door.

8. That you are surrounded by your family.

9. That things work out the way you want them to.

10. And that you have the happiest birthday ever!

— Ashley Rice

A Little
"Birthday Wisdom"
to keep in Your Heart

If a star twinkles... wish on it. When you spot a rainbow... search for the gold. Walk on the sunny side; dream on a cloud. Always remember that life is meant to be enjoyed.

Be gracious... angels are watching. Unfold your wings; rise and soar. Fill your life with wonder and your days with beauty. Set your dreams on the farthest star.

rainbow

angels

miracles

When you're caught between a rock and a hard place... plant a seed. Chart your course; map out your future. Sail away on your own cruise line, and remember there's no limit to how far you can go.

Believe in miracles. Look for silver linings. When the going gets tough... let faith smooth the way. Dreams come in all shapes and sizes. Do the things that warm your soul. Inspire yourself. Make good things happen. In every tomorrow a new promise shines.

Believe in yourself. Honor your strengths. A little hope and determination can overcome anything. Life is a candle... and you're its spark. Soar high and far. Open your arms and let life's good things come in. There are some spectacular moments designed for you — and no one is more deserving than you.

— Linda E. Knight

Take a Moment
Out of Your Day to Reflect,
Appreciate, and Be Grateful

Today is about you, so look around and smile at your life and your choices. Don't worry about the paths you should have taken or the opportunities you ignored. Instead, breathe in the life that surrounds you — let it fill your soul with light and hope.

Your beauty and wisdom have inspired, encouraged, soothed, and strengthened the people around you. Reflect on the past and all the memories, good and bad, that have made you who you are today. Your journey is far from over, as you will continue to grow, change, and flourish.

beauty

Life can be so busy, and we sometimes take for granted the important little things that make us smile. Look at the sunset, share a cup of coffee with your best friend, or hear the wind rustle through the trees. Take some time to listen to life and feel the sun on your face. Stop to watch butterflies in your garden.

Today, I give you the gifts of beauty, inspiration, love, and reflection. Use them wisely and carry them with you as you enter another year ahead.

— Carol Schelling

To describe you as being
"absolutely wonderful"
and "incredibly special"
doesn't even begin to convey
all the admiration
and appreciation
I have for you.
The world is a nicer place
with you in it,
and it is such a blessing
to have you here…
in my life and in the lives
of so many others…
brightening up so many days!

incredible

wonderful

You're just the best,
and your birthday is
a great chance
to tell you so.
I know the year ahead
will be a good one for you,
and I hope the joys and dreams
and things you wish for...
all come true.

— Terry Bairnson

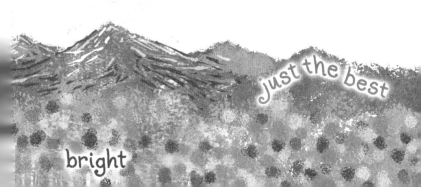

just the best

bright

Happy Birthday
to an Incredibly Kind, Caring, and Wise Soul

May the light you bring into the world always be reflected back to you, and may the love you share so easily be returned to you a thousand times over.

May you always see rainbows after dark storms. May you greet each rising of the sun with fresh eyes, knowing what it means to live a life full of wonder.

Stars

Moon

May you savor the stars and moon at night, and may you continue to wish upon shooting stars, the way you did as a child.

May you always be surrounded with hearts that love, arms that hug, and people who understand you and embrace each and every miracle you are fortunate enough to experience.

And with another year behind you, may you always know just how loved you are.

— Lamisha Serf-Walls

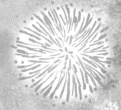

Happy
Birthday
to You!